W9-BYH-803

Welcome to Rainbow Bridge Publishing's Connection series. Reading Connection provides students with focused practice to help reinforce and develop reading skills in areas appropriate for first-grade students. Reading Connection uses a variety of writing types and exercises to help build comprehension, thinking, phonics, vocabulary, language, reasoning, and other skills important to both reading and critical thinking. In accordance with NCTE (National Council of Teachers of English) standards, reading material and exercises are grade-level appropriate, and clear examples and instructions guide the lesson. Activities help students develop reading skills and give special attention to vocabulary development.

Dear Parents and Educators,

Thank you for choosing this Rainbow Bridge Publishing educational product to help teach your children and students. We take great pride and pleasure in becoming involved with your educational experience. Some people say that math will always be math and reading will always be reading, but we do not share that opinion. Reading, math, spelling, writing, geography, science, history, and all other subjects will always be some of life's most fulfilling adventures and should be taught with passion both at home and in the classroom. Because of this, we at Rainbow Bridge Publishing associate the greatness of learning with every product we create.

It is our mission to provide materials that not only explain, but also amaze; not only review, but also encourage; not only guide, but also lead. Every product contains clear, concise instructions, appropriate sample work, and engaging, grade-appropriate content created by classroom teachers and writers that is based on national standards to support your best educational efforts. We hope you enjoy our company's products as you _____ Thank you for bringing us along.

Sincerely,

George Starks
Rainbow Bridge Publishing

Re
Written

MOFFATT
2 of each
2 Sided

Green

THX!

Series Creator
Michele Van Leeuwen

Illustrations
Amanda Sorensen

Visual Design and Layout
Andy Carlson, Robyn Funk

Editorial Director
Paul Rawlins

Copy Editors and Proofreaders
Kim Carlson, Suzie Ellison, Lori Davis

Special Thanks
Dante J. Orazzi

Please visit our website at
www.summerbridgeactivities.com
for supplements, additions, and corrections to this book.

Second Edition 2004

ISBN: 1-887923-80-2

PRINTED IN THE UNITED STATES OF AMERICA
10 9 8 7 6 5 4

Table of Contents

1st Grade Reading List

Ackerman, Karen
Song and Dance Man

Ahlberg, Janet
Funnybones

Allard, Harry
Miss Nelson Is Missing

Andersen, Hans Christian (retold by Anne Rockwell)
The Emperor's New Clothes

Arnold, Tedd
No Jumping on the Bed

Bemelmans, Ludwig
Madeline

Brown, Marcia
Stone Soup: An Old Tale

Capucilli, Alyssa Satin
Mrs. McTats and Her Houseful of Cats

Choi, Yangsook
The Name Jar

Cohen, Barbara
Molly's Pilgrim

Cosgrove, Stephen
Leo the Lop—I, II, III
Hucklebug
Morgan and Me
Kartusch
Snaffles

Dicks, Terrance
Adventures of Goliath

Dorros, Arthur
Abuela

Duvoisin, Roger
Petunia
Veronica

Ehlert, Lois
Market Day

Freeman, Don
Corduroy

Grimm, Jacob
The Frog Prince

Hall, Donald
Ox-Cart Man

Hutchins, Pat
Don't Forget the Bacon!
Good Night Owl!
Rosie's Walk

Isadora, Rachel
My Ballet Class

Kellogg, Steven
Paul Bunyon, a Tall Tale

Leaf, Munro
The Story of Ferdinand
Wee Gillis

Lobel, Arnold
Frog and Toad series

McCaughrean, Geraldine
Saint George and the Dragon

McCloskey, Robert
Make Way for Ducklings

Minarik, Else Holmelund
Little Bear

Park, Barbara
Junie B. Jones books

Peet, Bill
The Ant and the Elephant
Big Bad Bruce
Buford, the Little Bighorn
The Caboose Who Got Loose
Jethro and Joel Were a Troll

Rylant, Cynthia
Henry and Mudge books

Schwartz, Alvin
In a Dark, Dark Room

Sendak, Maurice
Higglety, Pigglety Pop!
Where the Wild Things Are

Sharmat, Marjorie Weinman
Nate the Great and the Musical Note

Slobodkina, Esphyr
Caps for Sale

Steig, William
Gorky Rises

Steptoe, John
Mufaro's Beautiful Daughters

Thomas, Shelley Moore
Good Night, Good Knight

Viorst, Judith
Alexander and the Terrible, Horrible, No Good, Very Bad Day

Waber, Bernard
Ira Sleeps Over

Ward, Lynd
The Biggest Bear

Yolen, Jane
Picnic with Piggins

Sounds and Letters Chart

rat ă	ape ā	snail ā	crayfish ā
bear b	cat c	centipede s	cheetah ch
deer d	elephant ě	seal ē	bee ē
fish f	gorilla g	giraffe j	horse h
inchworm ĭ	crocodile ī	jaguar j	kangaroo k
lion l	mouse m	newt n	gong ng

Sounds and Letters Chart

dog ŏ	goat ō	stone ō	goose o͞o
wood o͝o	crow ō	pig p	quail kw
rabbit r	skunk s	shark sh	turtle t
thrust th	duck ŭ	Duke ū	vulture v
wolf w	whale wh	Fox x	xylophone z
yak y	fly ī	pony ē	zebra z

Mole was not bold. He was shy. He liked to hide in his hole by the road. Toad hopped by Mole's home. He saw a moat all around Mole's home. Toad poked at the moat. It was wet and cold. Toad called, "Hello, Mole! Do I see a moat?"

Mole froze in his hole. He had a boat to sail in his moat. He did not want old Toad to know. A wet Toad would soak his boat. Again Toad shouted, "Hello! Do I see a boat for your moat?" Shy Mole wrote a note. He took a long pole. He poked the note up the hole. Toad read the note. It said, "Go away!" It was no joke. Toad sadly hopped down the road.

Next, Goat loped down the road. He saw Mole's home. He saw the moat. He did not care about the moat or the boat. He wanted to eat. He yelled down the hole, "I want to eat! Do you have some roast beef on toast?" This time Mole was more bold. He told that old goat, "O.K. Have half a loaf, but don't choke!"

Goat told Mole, "You are a very good host!"

After lunch, Mole went for a float on his boat in the moat.

Reading Skills

1. What is the main idea of the story?

   A. Mole was not bold. He was shy.

   B. Toad was not bold. He was shy.

   C. Goat was not bold. He was shy.

2. Why didn't Mole want Toad to know about his boat?

   A. Toad would hide in the boat.

   B. Toad would soak his boat.

   C. Toad would croak in the boat

3. What did Goat want from Mole?

   A. roast beef on toast

   B. gold

   C. to play

Vocabulary Skills

1. What is another word for <u>loped</u>?

   A. crawled

   B. slid

   C. ran

2. What is the meaning of the word <u>host</u> in this story?

   A. someone who takes care of a guest

   B. a place for another animal to live

   C. a large number

Language Skills

1. Put the long <u>o</u> words in the right row.

bold	hope	cold
boat	froze	note
road	moat	roast
choke	told	old

o_e

oa

old

Duke and the Mule

Duke was a dude who lived in the city.

He visited a ranch.

He tried to ride a mule.

The mule was rude.

It did not move.

Duke was not happy.

He sang a tune.

The mule did not like it.

Duke fed the mule.

He gave it a sugar cube.

The mule was happy.

It gave Duke a ride.

Reading Skills

1. What did Duke want to do?

   A. sing a song

   B. rope a horse

   C. ride a mule

   D. feed a cow

2. What did the mule not like?

   A. Duke's song

   B. sugar

   C. hay

   D. work

3. Why did the mule give Duke a ride?

   A. He gave the mule a carrot.

   B. He gave the mule a sugar cube.

   C. He gave the mule an apple.

   D. He gave the mule water.

4. What did the mule do when Duke tried to ride him?

   A. It trotted away.

   B. It laid down.

   C. It ran away.

   D. It did not move.

Vocabulary Skills

5. What is a dude?

   A. a dancer

   B. a farmer

   C. a person from the city who goes to a ranch

Language Skills

6. Write the six words from the story that follow the v-c-v rule, u_e. (v-c-v stands for vowel-con-sonant-vowel)

_____

_____

_____

_____

_____

_____

_____

_____

Ruby and her friends did a music show. The show was in July. Judy played a tune on her flute. Hugo played the bugle. Luke marched in his new uniform. Susan danced in her cute tutu. June and Ruby played a duet on their lutes. Duke played his huge tuba to end the show. Ruby said her friends were all super!

Reading Skills

1. What is the main idea of this story?

    A. a music show

    B. playing the tuba

    C. her cute tutu

2. Match the instrument to the person who played it.

June	tuba
Hugo	lute
Judy	bugle
Duke	flute

Language Skills

1. Write three long u words from the story.

_____

_____

_____

_____

2. Circle three more long u words in the story with the v-c-v pattern (v-c-v stands for vowel-consonant-vowel).

3. Find and circle the long u word in the story that does not follow the v-c-v pattern. Write it below.

_____

_____

Dawn, the Zookeeper

Dawn is a zookeeper. Her job is to keep the animals safe and happy. She cleans the cages and gives the animals clean straw. Last week a hawk began to squawk. Dawn saw that it had a sore claw. She called a vet to fix the hawk's claw. Another time, two of the big cats got in a brawl over raw meat. One cat got a hurt paw. The other cat had a sore jaw. Dawn took care of the big cats. Dawn loves animals. Dawn loves her job.

www.summerbridgeactivities.com **Reading Connection—Grade 1—RBP3802**

Reading Skills

1. Which sentence best tells the main idea of the story?

    A. Dawn takes care of the animals at the zoo.

    B. Dawn is safe and happy.

    C. The animals like Dawn.

2. What is a zookeeper's job?

    A. to only play with the animals.

    B. to only feed the animals.

    C. to keep the animals safe and happy.

3. What happened to the hawk?

    A. It had a sore claw.

    B. It was hungry.

    C. It couldn't fly.

4. What happened to the big cats?

    A. They wanted water.

    B. They got in a brawl.

    C. They didn't like each other.

Vocabulary Skills

1. What does <u>brawl</u> mean?

    A. cage

    B. fight

    C. game

Language Skills

1. Write eight <u>aw</u> words from the story.

_____

_____

_____

_____

_____

_____

_____

_____

My friend and I are way up high,
watching as the world goes by
from our tree house.

Down below on the ground,
little people move around
below our tree house.

Birds fly above and below us.
They screech and make a fuss
around our tree house.

www.summerbridgeactivities.com Reading Connection—Grade 1—RBP3802

Reading Skills

1. Which sentence tells the main idea of the poem?

   A. People on the ground are little.

   B. Birds fly in the sky.

   C. It is fun to play in a tree house.

2. What two people are in the tree house?

   A. a boy and a girl

   B. my friend and I

   C. two boys

3. How do the people on the ground look from the tree house?

   A. like big people

   B. like little people

   C. like giants

Thinking Skills

1. Why are the people little?

   A. They are children.

   B. They are short.

   C. They look little from up high.

Language Skills

1. Write four <u>ou</u> words from the poem.

_____

_____

_____

_____

Vocabulary Skills

1. What does <u>screech</u> mean?

   A. to circle around

   B. to make a loud sound

   C. to fly around

Reading Connection—Grade 1—RBP3802   www.summerbridgeactivities.com   ©RBP Books

A long time ago, there lived a boy named Troy. Troy dreamed of becoming a hero. There was also an evil wizard. He planned to steal the royal coin. The king heard of this evil plan. He said that anyone who could stop the evil wizard would be a hero. Troy had to try to foil the wizard's plan. Troy waited outside the castle. When he saw the wizard, he nabbed him. He coiled the wizard in a rope. The plan to steal the royal coin was foiled. The king was overjoyed. Troy became a hero.

Reading Skills

1. What could be another title for this story?

    A. The King Is a Hero

    B. Troy Becomes a Hero

    C. The Wizard Becomes a Hero

2. What did the wizard plan to do?

    A. become king

    B. turn Troy into a frog

    C. steal the royal coin

3. Why did Troy want to foil the plan?

    A. He wanted to become a hero.

    B. He didn't like the wizard.

    C. The king asked Troy to help.

4. How did Troy foil the wizard?

    A. He showed him the castle.

    B. He asked the king to help.

    C. He coiled him in a rope.

Language Skills

1. Put the words in groups.

boy	Troy	foil
royal	coil	coin

oi words	oy words
_____	_____
_____	_____
_____	_____
_____	_____
_____	_____

Vocabulary Skills

1. What does <u>foil</u> mean?

    A. to ruin

    B. to help

    C. to save

2. What does <u>overjoyed</u> mean?

    A. very happy

    B. scared

    C. angry

Reading Connection—Grade 1—RBP3802   www.summerbridgeactivities.com   ©RBP Books

When the cat fell in the pool, the Zoo Crew knew what to do.
They threw a loop.

When the goose threw the broom, the Zoo Crew knew what to do.
They ducked!

When the giraffe blew his nose, the Zoo Crew knew what to do.
They stood back!

When the hen flew the coop, the Zoo Crew knew what to do!
They made soup.

When the cow jumped over the moon, the Zoo Crew knew what to do.
They laughed.

www.summerbridgeactivities.com   Reading Connection—Grade 1—RBP3802

Reading Skills

1. Does this story give you true or make-believe facts about working at a zoo?

_____
- - - - - - - - - - - - - - - - - - -
_____
_____
- - - - - - - - - - - - - - - - - - -
_____
_____
- - - - - - - - - - - - - - - - - - -
_____
_____
- - - - - - - - - - - - - - - - - - -
_____

2. Draw a line between the problem and the solution.

cat fell in   they ducked
the pool

goose threw   they laughed
a broom

hen flew   they threw a loop
the coop

cow jumped   they made soup
over the moon

Language Skills

1. Group the words from the story. Find three words for each group.

<u>ew</u> words	<u>oo</u> words
_____	_____
_____	_____
_____	_____
_____	_____
_____	_____
_____	_____

Vocabulary Skills

1. A <u>coop</u> is a home for what kind of animal?
   A. cat
   B. cow
   C. giraffe
   D. hen

2. What is another word for "loop"?
   A. a straight rope
   B. lasso
   C. string

Captain Hook

Captain Hook, on sea or land,
  Had to do without a hand.

Captain Hook would shake his hook
  At the poor and timid cook.

"Catch a fish fresh from the brook,
While I read my brand-new book!"

    The timid cook went to the wood
    To catch a fish the best he could.

  He fished and fished, and hooked but one.
  Cook shook his head. "My time is done!"

    The fish he took to Captain Hook
    Was overcooked and full of soot.

  Hook put his book down near his foot,
  Then shook his hook at the poor cook.

"This fish is small and cooked too much.
  Look at the soot! I can't eat such stuff!"

That mean old Hook! He took his book
  And tossed it at the timid cook!

Reading Skills

1. What is the main idea of this poem?

    A. The cook went into the wood.

    B. Captain Hook was not a nice man.

    C. The poor, timid cook shook and shook.

2. Why didn't Captain Hook like the fish?

    A. The fish was too small.

    B. The fish wasn't cooked.

    C. The fish was overcooked and full of soot.

3. What did Captain Hook do when the cook gave him a fish?

    A. Captain Hook threw his book at the cook.

    B. Captain Hook read a new book.

    C. Captain Hook shook his hook.

Vocabulary Skills

1. What is another word for <u>soot</u>?

    A. ashes

    B. paper

    C. coal

2. What is another word for <u>timid</u>?

    A. brave

    B. loud

    C. shy

Language Skills

1. Write six <u>oo</u> words from the story.

_____   _____

_____   _____

_____   _____

_____   _____

_____   _____

_____   _____

Cody loves to make things from trash. Today he made a boat from a bar of soap. He used a stick, a rope, and some paper for the sail. Then Cody took the boat to the pond. He wanted to see if it would float. He put the boat into the water. It did float! Cody was proud. Suddenly, a little toad jumped from the shore onto the boat. The toad sat proudly upon the boat.

www.summerbridgeactivities.com

Reading Skills

1. What is the main idea of the story?

    A. A toad jumps on the boat.

    B. The boat could float.

    C. Cody made a boat.

2. Draw a line from the question to the answer.

Who?	at the pond
What?	sailed a boat
When?	Cody
Where?	today

3. Circle the things that Cody used to make his boat.

soap   rope   tape   toad

      paper   stick

Thinking Skills

1. What do you think Cody might make next?

_____

_____

_____

_____

Language Skills

1. Group the words.

love   soap   toad

float   rope   shore

oa words	o-e words

Vocabulary Skills

1. What does <u>proud</u> mean?

    A. feeling good about yourself

    B. feeling scared about something

    C. feeling sad about something

Reading Connection—Grade 1—RBP3802   www.summerbridgeactivities.com   © RBP Books

Jan and Jane are twins. They like to play hide-and-seek. Jan hid first. She hid in a big can. Jane tapped the can with a cane. Jan came out. Now it was Jane's turn to hide. She hid behind a big cube. It was easy for Jan to see her. Pete came by with his toy bear cub. He was sad. His bear cub had a cut on its paw. Jan and Jane thought the cub was cute. They hoped the bear cub could be mended. They waved good-bye to Pete and his pet. They did not want to play hide-and-seek anymore. They decided to play hopscotch. Jan and Jane had a fun afternoon.

Reading Skills

1. What was wrong with Pete's toy bear cub?

    A. It was sick.

    B. It had a cut on its paw.

    C. It was old.

2. Put the events from the story in order.

    ____ playing hide-and-seek

    ____ playing hopscotch

    ____ seeing Pete and his pet

Vocabulary Skills

1. What is another word for <u>mended</u>?

    A. torn

    B. ripped

    C. fixed

Language Skills

1. Change the short vowel words to long vowel words by adding a silent <u>e</u> to the word.

Jan _____

hid _____

tap _____

cub _____

pet _____

cut _____

hop _____

Reading Connection—Grade 1—RBP3802 www.summerbridgeactivities.com ©RBP Books

I
love
spring more
than anything.
More than anything,
I love spring.

I like to sing in the spring
about the flowers spring brings,
and how I wish
I were a bird with wings.

I like to hold a kite
by its string
and fly on a swing.
I feel like a king
in the
spring.

www.summerbridgeactivities.com **Reading Connection—Grade 1—RBP3802**

Reading Skills

1. Which sentence tells the main idea of the poem?

   A. There is a lot to love about spring.

   B. Spring comes after winter.

   C. Birds fly in the spring.

2. What does the child sing about?

   A. flowers

   B. buds

   C. kites

3. When does the child like to hold a kite by its string?

   A. while running

   B. while flying on a swing

   C. while skipping

4. Circle the things the writer of the poem loves about spring.

singing   rainbows

kite flying   baby animals

flowers   swings

Thinking Skills

1. What is your favorite season?

_____

_____

Write two things you like about that season.

_____

_____

_____

_____

Vocabulary Skills

1. What does it mean to "feel like a king"?

   A. to feel sad

   B. to feel great

   C. to feel silly

What Do You Think?

Should you drink pink ink?
I don't think so.

Should you blink if someone shoots you with some ink?
Yes, I think so.

Should you spit on a rink?
I don't think so.

Should you link a chain around the rink?
Yes, I think so.

Should you shrink your mother's mink?
I don't think so.

Should you clean your mother's mink if it stinks?
Yes, I think so.

www.summerbridgeactivities.com Reading Connection—Grade 1—RBP3802

Reading Skills

1. Which sentence tells the main idea of the poem.

    A. Think about what you do.

    B. Don't drink pink ink.

    C. Link a chain around a rink.

2. Put a √ by the things you should do and an X by the things you shouldn't do.

    ____ drink pink ink

    ____ spit on a rink

    ____ link a chain around a rink

    ____ clean your mother's mink

    ____ blink if someone shoots you with ink

    ____ shrink your mother's mink

Thinking Skills

1. Make a list of things you should do.

Vocabulary Skills

1. Write five -ink words from the poem.

Language Skills

1. Circle the nk words in the story. Choose four nk words to write.

Reading Connection—Grade 1—RBP3802   www.summerbridgeactivities.com   © RBP Books

Please come here so you can hear.
Can't you see the deer, my dear?

Please come to the sea to see
if a flea can really flee.

Please come to school to learn to write right
and to add two plus two, too.
Maybe next week if you're not still feeling weak
from the flu.

www.summerbridgeactivities.com

Thinking Skills

1. Circle Yes or No to answer each question.

Are you learning to write right?
Yes   No

Have you been to the sea to see?
Yes   No

Can a flea flee?
Yes   No

Can you add two plus two, too?
Yes   No

Can you see a deer, my dear?
Yes   No

Vocabulary Skills

1. Circle the correct word in each sentence.

Fish swim in the (see / sea).

A mother (deer / dear) is called a doe.

I can (see / sea) you.

My mother calls me (deer / dear).

2. Draw a line between the words that sound the same but have different meanings.

flu   wear

ate   weak

there   flew

where   their

week   eight

Language Skills

1. Put the words <u>same</u> and <u>different</u> in the sentence so that the sentence is true:

Homonyms are words that sound

_____

the _____ but have

_____ meanings.

Thinking Skills

1. Think of two more homonyms and write them.

_____

_____

_____

_____

It's a time to read and a time to sleep.
It's a time to think and a time to weep.

It's a time to let your imagination run.
It's a time to plan how to get things done.

It's a time to sit and be alone.
It's a time to be thankful for all you own.

It's a time to watch a little ant.
It's a time to say, "I can," not "can't."

It's a time to think about movies, books, and plays.
It's a time to remember all your yesterdays.

Quiet time is a special time,
but often overlooked.
We forget to have some quiet time
when we're overbooked.

Reading Skills

1. Which sentence tells the main idea of the poem?

   A. Quiet time is boring.

   B. Quiet time is a special time for thinking.

   C. Quiet time is better than recess.

2. Circle the sentence that is not true about quiet times.

   Quiet time can be for taking a nap.

   Quiet time can be for reading.

   Quiet time is a good time to think.

   Quiet time is only at night when it's really quiet.

Thinking Skills

1. What do you like to do during a quiet time?

   _____
   _____
   _____
   _____
   _____
   _____
   _____

Vocabulary Skills

1. Write the two words that make up each contraction.

   it's   _____
            _____

   can't   _____
            _____

   we're   _____
            _____

Denise and Her Kite

Denise got a new kite.

It was blue and red with white spots.

Denise wanted to fly her kite.

She went outside.

The wind was blowing.

She went up a hill.

She ran fast down the hill.

Her kite went up and up, high in the sky.

Denise had fun flying her new kite.

Reading Skills

1. Draw a picture of Denise's kite.

2. What did Denise want to do?

3. Where did Denise go to fly her kite?

Language Skills

1. Circle the long i words.

Denise   kit   white   kite

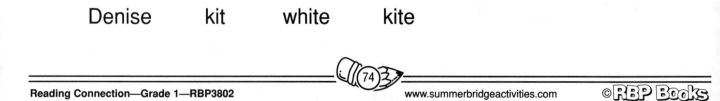

Reading Connection—Grade 1—RBP3802   www.summerbridgeactivities.com   © RBP Books

Mary woke up early. Mom and Dad were asleep. She wanted to surprise them. Mary dressed herself. She combed her hair and went downstairs.

Mary put some cereal in two bowls. She added some milk. She made toast with jam. Mary put the food on a tray. She took it up the stairs to Mom and Dad. They were surprised to have breakfast in bed.

Reading Skills

1. How did Mary surprise Mom and Dad?

_____

- -

_____

2. Number the sentences in the order they happened in the story.

___ She made toast with jam.

___ She combed her hair and went downstairs.

___ Mary woke up early.

___ They were surprised to have breakfast in bed.

3. What did Mary put on the toast?

_____

- -

_____

Thinking Skills

1. How did Mom and Dad feel about breakfast in bed?

_____

- -

_____

_____

- -

_____

_____

- -

_____

"It's time," my mother always says.
"It's time for what?" I reply.
"It's always time for something."
"Oh my, how time can fly."

It's time to rise.
It's time to eat.
It's time to go to sleep.

It's time to dance.
It's time to play.
It's time to jump and leap.

It's time to be nice.
It's time to be sweet.
It's time to learn to write.

It's time to go out.
It's time to come in.
It's time to turn on the light.

It's time to be you.
It's time to be me.
Let's be friends. It's time.

www.summerbridgeactivities.com   **Reading Connection—Grade 1—RBP3802**

Reading Skills

1. Which sentence tells the main idea of this poem?

   A. It is always time for some-thing.

   B. Mothers like to nag.

   C. You should always do your best.

Thinking Skills

1. What do you like to do with your time?

_____

_____

_____

_____

_____

_____

_____

_____

_____

_____

_____

Language Skills

1. Group the words.

time	leap	rise
eat	sweet	nice
light	fly	me
write	sleep	

long e words	long i words

Vocabulary Skills

1. What does <u>reply</u> mean?

   A. answer

   B. sing

   C. listen

www.summerbridgeactivities.com ©RBP Books

Look for colors all around.
What colors of a rainbow can be found?

Green is found in the grasshopper hopping around the lake.
Brown is found in the syrup on my pancake.

Red is found in Superman's cape.
Purple is found in a vineyard grape.

Blue is found in a blueberry pie.
Orange is found in a clown's bow tie.

Yellow is found in a sunflower.
Black is found at the midnight hour.

Colors of the rainbow can be found,
if you'll only take the time to look around.

©RBP Books www.summerbridgeactivities.com Reading Connection—Grade 1—RBP3802

Reading Skills

1. Which sentence tells the main idea of the poem?

    A. Rainbows are very pretty.

    B. Rainbows come out after the rain.

    C. Colors can be found all around us.

    D. Red and blue are pretty colors.

2. Write the pairs of rhyming words used in this poem.

around and _____

lake and _____

cape and _____

pie and _____

sunflower and _____

Thinking Skills

1. What is your favorite color? Name three things that are the same color.

_____

_____

_____

_____

_____

_____

_____

_____

Vocabulary Skills

1. Draw a line between the two words in each compound word.

blue	hopper
sun	night
grass	bow
pan	flower
rain	man
mid	cake
Super	berry
vine	yard

Sparky is the name of my new dog. Dad gave him to me for my birthday. He is black with a white spot around one eye. I take care of him. I see that he has food and water. I fixed a warm place for him to sleep.

Sparky and I have fun. We play ball. I toss the ball. He brings it back. I hide from him. He finds me. We like to race. When I come home from school, he is there to meet me. It is fun having my own dog.

www.summerbridgeactivities.com   Reading Connection—Grade 1—RBP3802

Reading Skills

1. What is this story mostly about?

    A. a sad surprise

    B. a pet dog

    C. a sad boy

    D. a sad dog

2. What can Sparky do?

    A. shake hands

    B. walk on his back legs

    C. bring back a ball

    D. play in the park

3. Who gave Sparky to the child?

    A. Mom

    B. Dad

    C. a friend

    D. a brother

4. What does the child not do to care for the dog?

    A. cut the dog's hair

    B. feed the dog

    C. give the dog water

    D. give the dog a warm place

Vocabulary Skills

1. In the story the word spot means a _____.

    A. a mark

    B. a color

    C. stop

    D. a ball

Thinking Skills

1. You can guess that Sparky is _____.

    A. a good boy

    B. a good pet

    C. a fast runner

    D. a bad dog

2. If you have a dog or got one for a present, what tricks would you teach your dog?

_____

- - - - - - - - - - - - - - - - - - -

_____

_____

- - - - - - - - - - - - - - - - - - -

_____

_____

- - - - - - - - - - - - - - - - - - -

_____

It was a hot summer day. "This is a good day to be lazy. I will lie in the shade of the apple tree," said Billy.

Soon, Katie came skipping by. "What are you doing?" she asked.

"Oh, nothing," replied Billy.

"I think I'll do nothing, too," said Katie. She sat down next to Billy.

They saw an ant pulling a big leaf. A ladybug flew onto Katie's hand. A grasshopper hopped by. A bee landed on a flower. "It is fun doing nothing," said Billy and Katie.

www.summerbridgeactivities.com **Reading Connection—Grade 1—RBP3802**

Reading Skills

1. Which sentence tells the main idea of this story?

    A. An ant pulled a big leaf

    B. It was a hot summer day.

    C. Billy and Katie sat under an apple tree.

    _____

2. A _____ flew onto Katie's hand.

3. Match the insects to what they did in the story.

hopped by	bee
flew onto Katie's hand	grasshopper
pulled a big leaf	ladybug
landed on a flower	ant

Thinking Skills

1. What do you like to do on a hot summer day?

_____

_____

_____

_____

Allie likes to play dress-up. She likes to dress as a bride. Allie will put on a long white dress and drape a pretty shawl on her head. She even has some roses. Sometimes she will put on her big sister's dance outfit. Then she will do a dance. Allie also thinks it is fun to be a clown. She will put on her dad's big shoes and color her nose red.

Allie likes playing Mom best. She dresses up in her mom's clothes. She takes her bag and shops for food in the kitchen pantry. Her doll is always her baby. She feeds her baby. Then she sings her baby to sleep.

Playing dress-up is lots of fun.

Reading Skills

1. What is the main idea of this story?

    A. Allie likes to dress up as a bride.

    B. Playing dress-up is lots of fun.

    C. Allie likes to dress up as a clown.

2. What does Allie like dressing up as best?

    A. Mom

    B. a dancer

    C. a clown

3. Put the events from the story in order.

    ____ playing Mom

    ____ being a clown

    ____ being a bride

    ____ being a dancer

Thinking Skills

1. Who is your favorite person to dress up as? Why?

_____

_____

_____

_____

_____

_____

_____

_____

_____

_____

_____

_____

Vocabulary Skills

1. What does the word <u>drape</u> mean in the story?

    A. curtains

    B. to cover loosely

    C. to wrap tightly

One warm spring day, the ducklings decided to go to the pond. The ducklings wanted to go for a swim.

"Can we go, too?" asked the chicks.

"Chicks cannot swim," laughed the ducklings.

"We will run in the tall grass and look for bugs. Please let us come." So the ducklings and the chicks set off to the pond.

The ducklings swam in the pond. They splashed in the water. The chicks ran in the tall grass. They looked for bugs. The ducklings and the chicks had lots of fun. After a while, the ducklings and chicks were tired. They were <u>exhausted</u> from playing hard. They missed their mothers. They missed their nests. It was time to go home.

Reading Skills

1. Which sentence tells the main idea of the story?

   A. Ducklings have fun swimming.

   B. Chicks and ducklings hatch from eggs.

   C. Both ducklings and chicks can have fun at the pond.

2. Number the sentences in the order they happened in the story.

   ____ It was time to go home.

   ____ The ducklings wanted to go to the pond.

   ____ The ducklings swam in the pond while the chicks ran in the grass.

   ____ The ducklings and the chicks got tired.

3. Put a **T** by the sentences that are true. Put an **F** by the sentences that are false.

   ____ The chicks swam in the pond.

   ____ The ducklings swam in the pond.

   ____ The ducklings looked for bugs.

   ____ Both the ducklings and chicks missed their mothers.

Vocabulary Skills

1. What does <u>exhausted</u> mean?

   A. tired

   B. silly

   C. happy

   D. angry

Reading Connection—Grade 1—RBP3802

One day Fox was busy making something. Turtle came by.

"What are you making, Fox?" asked Turtle. "Nothing," answered Fox. "It looks like a trap to me," said Turtle as he strolled away.

Soon Mouse came by. "What are you making, Fox?" asked Mouse. "Nothing," answered Fox. "It looks like a trap to me," said Mouse as he scampered away.

Before long, Duck came by. "What are you making, Fox?" asked Duck. "Nothing," answered Fox. "It looks like a trap to me," said Duck as he waddled away.

Just as Fox finished, Rabbit came by. "What did you make, Fox?" asked Rabbit. "A home for a rabbit," Fox said. "It looks like a trap to me," said Rabbit. "Nonsense," said Fox. "Come closer and have a look." "But I don't think I will fit," said Rabbit.

"Nonsense," said Fox. "It's big enough for me." Fox crawled inside. With Fox inside, Rabbit shut the latch. The door shut tight. Rabbit hopped off, saying, "It looks like a trap to me."

Reading Skills

1. Which sentence best tells the main idea of the story?

    A. Fox built a trap for himself.

    B. Fox is very busy.

    C. Fox built a home for Rabbit.

2. What got caught in Fox's trap?

    A. the turtle

    B. the mouse

    C. the fox

    D. the rabbit

3. Put a number by the animals in the order that they met Fox.

    ____ Rabbit

    ____ Turtle

    ____ Mouse

    ____ Duck

Thinking Skills

1. Why did Fox want to make a trap?

    A. He liked to build things.

    B. He wanted to catch Rabbit.

    C. He had extra wood.

2. Why do you think the fox always said, "nothing," when others asked what he was making?

_____

_____

_____

_____

_____

_____

Vocabulary Skills

1. Draw the line between the animal and how it moved.

turtle	scampered
mouse	hopped
duck	strolled
rabbit	waddled

Grayson and the Dragon

Once upon a time, to be important you had to slay a dragon. Grayson did not want to slay a dragon. He just liked to play. But Grayson wanted to be important. So he went to find a dragon.

Soon, he came to an old, gray palace. Grayson shouted, "Is there a dragon home?"

"Yes," answered the dragon. The dragon began to huff and puff. He blew until all his fire was gone.

The dragon began to cry. "What good is a dragon with no fire? Besides, I'm not a mean dragon. I'm a playful dragon. I just want to have fun."

"Me, too!" said Grayson. "Why don't you come home with me? We will play together." So Grayson became important. He was the only kid with his own dragon.

© RBP Books   www.summerbridgeactivities.com   Reading Connection—Grade 1—RBP3802

Reading Skills

1. Draw a line from the question to the answer.

Who?   once upon a time

What?   went to find a dragon

When?   Grayson

2. Why did the dragon start to cry?

     A. He was out of fire.

     B. Grayson hurt him.

     C. Dragons always cry.

3. How did Grayson come to feel important?

     A. He was the only kid with his own dragon.

     B. He owned a castle.

     C. He killed a dragon.

Vocabulary Skills

1. What does <u>important</u> mean?

     A. an adult

     B. special

     C. anyone, it doesn't matter who

Thinking Skills

1. "Once upon a time" tells you that the story is

     A. true

     B. make-believe

2. What would you do with a dragon?

_____

_____

_____

_____

_____

_____

_____

_____

_____

_____

My Dream

Last night I had a dream about being an astronaut. As I fell asleep, I found myself counting, "Ten, nine, eight … blastoff!" I dreamed I blasted into space.

I landed on Mars first. I raced in the red soil, making dust clouds behind me. Next, I played leapfrog on the moons of Jupiter. Then, I sailed around in the rings of Saturn. Suddenly, I began spinning out of control. Next thing I knew, I was on my bedroom floor.

I hope my dream comes true someday .

Reading Skills

1. Which title tells the main idea?

   A. Falling Out of Bed

   B. Playing Leapfrog in Space

   C. Dreaming about Being an Astronaut

   D. Space Is an Adventure

2. Draw a line from the planet to the word that tells something about the planet.

Mars	rings
Jupiter	red soil
Saturn	moons

3. Number the sentences in the order they happened in the dream.

   ____ I was on my bedroom floor.

   ____ I played leapfrog on the moons of Jupiter.

   ____ I dreamed I blasted into outer space.

   ____ I raced in the red soil.

Vocabulary Skills

1. Circle the two meanings of the word <u>dream</u>.

   A. thoughts you have when you are sleeping

   B. make-believe

   C. to tell a lie

   D. to hope for

Thinking Skills

1. Write about a dream you have had.

_____

_____

_____

_____

_____

_____

_____

_____

_____

_____

_____

_____

Once upon a time there were two little mice. One mouse lived under a vine outside a large house. The other mouse lived under the tile inside the large house.

The vine mouse liked to eat plain rice. The tile mouse liked to eat bites of fine food.

The vine mouse liked to play hide-and-seek outside. The tile mouse liked to sit inside.

The two mice were quite opposite. Still, the two mice were fine friends.

Reading Skills

1. Which sentence tells the lesson of this fable?

   A. Good friends can be different.

   B. Some mice like to have fun.

   C. Mice are different from cats.

2. Put a **T** by the sentences that are true. Put an **F** by the sentences that are false.

   ____ The vine mouse liked to eat bites of fine food.

   ____ The tile mouse liked to sit inside.

   ____ The two mice liked the same things.

   ____ The two mice were fine friends.

Thinking Skills

1. Which mouse do you think has the better life? Why?

_____

_____

_____

_____

_____

_____

2. Think about a friend. Write one way that you are like your friend. Write one way that you are not like your friend.

_____

_____

_____

_____

_____

_____

Vocabulary Skills

1. What does the word <u>opposite</u> mean?

   A. the same

   B. different

   C. good friends

Reading Connection—Grade 1—RBP3802   www.summerbridgeactivities.com   ©**RBP Books**

Birthday Candles

Birthday candles on the cake,
how many candles does it take?

One for baby sister, Jane.
Three for little brother, Cain.

Five for my funny cousin, Lee.
Almost seven, just for me.

Nine for my sister. Her name is Gail.
Ten for my oldest brother, Dale.

We saved a bunch for Mom and Dad.
Grandma needed all we had.

Birthday candles on the cake,
how many candles does it take?

Reading Skills

1. Which title best tells the main idea of this poem?

    A. Naming My Family

    B. Grandma and the Candles

    C. Counting Candles

2. Who needed all of the candles?

    A. Dad

    B. Mom

    C. Grandma

3. How many brothers and sisters does the writer of this poem have?

_____

_____

_____

Vocabulary Skills

1. What does <u>bunch</u> mean in this poem?

    A. a few

    B. a lot

    C. none

Language Skills

1. Group the words.

cake	Lee	me
take	Gail	three

long <u>a</u> words	long <u>e</u> words
_____	_____
_____	_____
_____	_____

Thinking Skills

1. How many candles will be on your birthday cake, and what kind of a cake will you have?

_____

_____

_____

_____

_____

_____

"Will you play hide-and-seek?" Jake asked his mother. "I don't have time. I have to find some tape," said Jake's mother. "I'll help," said Jake. He looked high and low. He found his mother's tape in a pile on her desk.

"Will you play hide-and-seek?" said Jake to his brother. "I don't have time. I have to find my kite," his brother said. "I'll help," Jake said. He looked high and low. He found his brother's kite by the gate.

"Will you play hide-and-seek?" said Jake to his father. "I don't have time. I have to find my rope," his father said. "I'll help," Jake said. He looked high and low. He found his father's rope by the rake.

"Will you play hide-and-seek?" Jake said to his sister. "I don't have time. I have to find my dime," his sister said. "I'll help," Jake said. He looked high and low. He found his sister's dime behind the drapes.

"Too bad no one has time to play hide-and-seek," laughed Jake.

www.summerbridgeactivities.com **Reading Connection—Grade 1—RBP3802**

Reading Skills

1. Which sentence tells the main idea of the story?

   A. Jake played hide-and-seek by finding things his family lost.

   B. Jake likes to play games with his family.

   C. Jake played hide-and-seek with his friends.

2. Draw a line from each member of Jake's family to the object he or she lost.

mother	rope
father	kite
sister	tape
brother	dime

3. What did Jake's brother have to find?

   A. a dime

   B. a rope

   C. a kite

4. Where did Jake find his mother's tape?

   A. by the gate

   B. on her desk

   C. behind the drapes

Thinking Skills

1. Why did Jake laugh when he said, "Too bad no one has time to play hide-and-seek"?

   A. He thought it was a joke.

   B. They played hide-and-seek looking for the things.

   C. He thought it was funny that his family kept losing things.

Vocabulary Skills

1. What does <u>drapes</u> mean?

   A. couch

   B. dresser

   C. curtains

Nate has a sailboat named <u>Wave Rider</u>. James is Nate's shipmate. Nate sails the boat. James keeps the boat clean and neat.

Nate and James like to sail whenever they can. Today they catch a big wave out to sea. Nate brags about the perfect day. Suddenly, it starts to rain.

The sea is no longer safe. The wind seems to scream, "Race to shore!" James and Nate sail the boat back to shore. They will wait for another day.

© RBP Books   www.summerbridgeactivities.com   Reading Connection—Grade 1—RBP3802

Reading Skills

1. Circle the headline that best tells the main idea.

    A. Boys Set Sail, Rain Sends Them Home

    B. The Sea Isn't Safe

    C. Boys Get Seasick

2. Why do the boys sail back to shore?

    A. It starts to rain.

    B. They are tired of sailing.

    C. They are in a race.

Vocabulary Skills

1. <u>Sailboat</u> and <u>shipmate</u> are compound words. Write the two little words that make up these words.

_____

_____

_____

_____

_____

_____

2. What does <u>shipmate</u> mean?

    A. a sailing friend

    B. a matching ship

    C. shipshape

Thinking Skills

1. Why is <u>Wave Rider</u> a good name for a boat?

_____

_____

_____

_____

_____

2. What would you name a boat? Why?

_____

_____

_____

_____

_____

_____

_____

What's in a cake, we ask?
Mom says it's an easy task.

Just follow this simple recipe,
And a yummy cake you will see.

Mom's Best White Cake

1 cup flour
1 cup sugar
1 teaspoon baking powder
1 teaspoon salt
1/2 cup butter
1 teaspoon vanilla
2 eggs

Heat oven to 350°.
Mix flour, sugar, baking powder, and salt.
Cream together butter, vanilla, and eggs.
Add flour mixture to the egg mixture and stir.
Pour into pan. Bake for 30 minutes.

What's in a cake, we ask?
Mom says it's an easy task.

We followed this simple recipe,
And a yummy cake we did see!

www.summerbridgeactivities.com   Reading Connection—Grade 1—RBP3802

Reading Skills

1. Which sentence best tells the main idea?

    A. Cake is my favorite dessert.

    B. Mom likes white cake best.

    C. You can follow a recipe to bake a cake.

2. Number the sentences in the order they happened in the recipe.

    ____ Add flour mixture to the egg mixture.

    ____ Heat oven to 350°.

    ____ Mix flour, sugar, baking powder, and salt.

    ____ Pour in pan.

    ____ Cream together butter, vanilla, and eggs.

3. How hot should the oven be to bake the cake?

    A. 450 degrees

    B. 250 degrees

    C. 350 degrees

Vocabulary Skills

1. Put a √ beside all the words that mean the same as mix.

    ____ stir

    ____ blend

    ____ chop

    ____ measure

2. What does the word task mean?

    A. recipe

    B. job

    C. question

3. What does the word cream mean in the recipe?

    A. the rich, yellowish part of milk

    B. to blend together

    C. a lotion

Thinking Skills

1. What is your favorite kind of cake? Why?

_____

_____

_____

_____

Fire Safety Rules

1. Don't play with matches.

2. If you see a fire:
   Tell an adult.
   Call 911.

3. If you are in a burning house:
   Don't hide.
   Keep low.
   Break a window if you have to.
   Don't open a hot door.

4. If you get fire on you, stop, drop, and roll.
   Stop what you are doing.
   Drop to the floor or ground.
   Roll around until the fire is out.

5. Talk with your family about a fire escape plan.

6. While camping:
   Use only fire spaces.
   Be sure the campfire is completely out before you leave or go
   to sleep.

©RBP Books   www.summerbridgeactivities.com   Reading Connection—Grade 1—RBP3802

Reading Skills

1. What could be another title for these rules?

   A. Keeping Safe at Home

   B. Keeping Safe from Fire

   C. Firemen to the Rescue

2. What does "Stop, drop, and roll" mean?

   A. Stop what you are doing, fall to the ground or floor, and roll.

   B. Stop at a friend's house, drop in, and ask for a roll.

   C. It's a new dance step.

3. When should you call 911?

   A. when you see a fire

   B. after school

   C. before you go to bed

4. Put an **X** by what you should do if there is a fire.

___ call a friend

___ call 911

___ open a hot door

___ hide

___ drop and roll

___ break a window if you have to

___ stop what you are doing

Thinking Skills

1. On another piece of paper, draw your own fire safety poster. Share it with your family.

Little Toad hopped out of the pond. "Where are you going, Little Toad?" asked the other toads. "I'm tired of living in this pond with so many toads," he said. "I need more room." So Little Toad hopped away.

Soon he met a rabbit. "Little Toad, why are you so far from home?" "I need more room," said Little Toad. "You can live with me. There is lots of room under the roots of this old tree." "No, thank you," said Little Toad. "This is no place for me."

Next he met a bee. When he told the bee his story, the bee buzzed, "You can not live with me. You would get stuck in my honey." Little Toad said, "Don't worry, bee, a honey tree is no place for me." Little Toad hopped away.

Then Little Toad met a dog. But before he could say a word, the dog barked and chased Little Toad away. "Living with a dog is not the place for me," thought Little Toad.

Little Toad hopped and hopped. Before he knew it, he had hopped all the way back to his pond. The other toads were happy to see him. They moved over to make room for him. Little Toad settled in and smiled, "Now this is the place for me."

Reading Skills

1. Which sentence tells the main idea of the story?

   A. A tree is no place for a toad.

   B. Dogs do not like toads.

   C. Little Toad finds out that home is best.

2. Number the sentences as they happened in the story.

   ____ Little Toad hopped all the way back to his pond.

   ____ Little Toad hopped out of the pond.

   ____ Little Toad met a rabbit.

   ____ Little Toad was chased by a dog.

   ____ Little Toad met a bee.

Language Skills

1. Write the past tense of each word. Circle the words in the story.

meet   _____

say   _____

think   _____

2. Write the words from the story that show past tense under the best heading.

add <u>ed</u>

_____
_____
_____
_____
_____
_____

double consonant and add <u>ed</u>

_____
_____

add <u>d</u> after silent <u>e</u>

_____
_____
_____
_____
_____
_____
_____

What do you want to know?

Do you want to know how long some seals can stay underwater?
Then read a book.

Do you want know what you call a group of wolves, a group of fish, or a group of whales? Then read a book.

Do you want to know why a rabbit is a rabbit and not a hare?
Then read a book.

Do you want to know what happens when an octopus is scared?
Then read a book.

Do you want to know how many rows of teeth a shark has? Then read a book.

What do you want to know?
Let's read a book!

Reading Skills

1. Which sentence tells the main idea?

   A. Read a book to find out whatever you want to know.

   B. Some seals can stay underwater.

   C. Animals are interesting.

2. Put an **X** by the things you could find out in a book.

   ____ how long seals stay underwater

   ____ what time dinner will be

   ____ facts about horses

   ____ how many rows of teeth a shark has

   ____ what your favorite color is

Thinking Skills

1. Do you like reading?

_____

_____

Why or why not?

_____

_____

_____

_____

2. Write a question. Use a book to find out the answer. Write the answer.

_____

_____

_____

_____

_____

_____

_____

_____

_____

_____

_____

_____

When is a sniffle just a sniffle, not a cold?
When is a germ just a germ, not a mold?

When is a cuddle just a cuddle, not a hug?
When is an ant just an ant, not a bug?

When is a bumble just a bumble, not a bee?
When is an apple just an apple, not a tree?

When is a giggle just a giggle, not a laugh?
When are bubbles just some bubbles, not a bath?

When is a battle just a battle, not a war?
When is an exit just an exit, not a door?

Reading Skills

1. Put an **X** beside the sentence that is **not** true about a riddle.

____ Riddles are questions.

____ Riddles can be found in a dictionary.

____ Riddles can be funny.

2. Draw lines between the words that go together.

sniffle   hug

cuddle   war

giggle   cold

battle   laugh

3. Match the rhyming words

cold   tree

hug   bug

bee   mold

Thinking Skills

1. Choose one of the questions from the poem and answer it.

_____

- - - - - - - - - - - - - - - - - - - -

_____

_____

- - - - - - - - - - - - - - - - - - - -

_____

_____

- - - - - - - - - - - - - - - - - - - -

_____

2. See if you can make up your own riddle.

_____

- - - - - - - - - - - - - - - - - - - -

_____

_____

- - - - - - - - - - - - - - - - - - - -

_____

_____

- - - - - - - - - - - - - - - - - - - -

_____

_____

- - - - - - - - - - - - - - - - - - - -

_____

Vocabulary Skills

1. What does <u>cuddle</u> mean?

A. to hug

B. to giggle

C. to laugh

My friends and I have no time to walk.
Instead, we…

prance like horses,
run like dogs,
hop like rabbits,
waddle like ducks,
frolic like lambs,
strut like roosters,
pace like hens, and
leap like frogs.

When we grow up, we'll have time to walk.

Reading Skills

1. What could be another title for this poem?

    A. Roosters Like to Strut

    B. Walk Like the Animals

    C. Growing Up

Vocabulary Skills

2. What does the word <u>strut</u> mean?

    A. to run as fast as you can

    B. to crawl

    C. to walk proudly

3. Put a √ beside the words for different ways to move.

    ____ prance

    ____ jump

    ____ waddle

    ____ strut

    ____ laugh

    ____ pace

4. Which do you think is faster, to strut or to run?

_____

_____

_____

_____

Thinking Skills

1. Why do you think the writer of this poem has no time to walk?

_____

_____

_____

_____

_____

_____

_____

_____

It is Halloween. All of the children are excited. Denise is a princess. Rob is a wizard. Allie is a clown. They go to the mall. Before the Trunk or Treat begins, the children show their costumes. They form a parade inside the mall. Everyone claps for the children.

Now, it is time for treats. They go outside. Cars are parked in a big circle. The car trunks are full of candy. The children are given candy from each car trunk. Soon, their sacks are full.

The snow starts to fall. It is getting cold. Denise, Rob, and Allie go home where it is warm. They count their candy. Denise thinks she has so much candy, it will last for a year.

www.summerbridgeactivities.com   **Reading Connection—Grade 1—RBP3802**

Reading Skills

1. Where do the children go for Trunk or Treat?

    A. their neighbors' houses

    B. their grandparents'

    C. the mall

2. What do the children do before the Trunk or Treat begins?

    A. They form a parade inside the mall.

    B. They give candy to their friends.

    C. They take off their costumes.

3. Match the children to their costumes.

Denise   wizard

Rob   clown

Allie   princess

4. How are the cars parked at the mall?

    A. in a square

    B. in a circle

    C. in a line

Thinking Skills

1. Draw a picture of your favorite Halloween costume.

Sammy Snail was sad. He wanted to run in the big race, but he was too slow. Robby Rabbit hopped up to Sammy Snail. "Why are you so sad?" he asked.

"I am too slow to be in the big race," cried Sammy Snail.

"Sammy Snail, you are too slow!" laughed Robby Rabbit as he hopped down the road.

Kami Kangaroo saw Sammy Snail on her way to the race. "Why are you crying?" she asked.

"I am too slow to run in the big race!" sobbed Sammy Snail.

"Don't cry. I will help you," said Kami Kangaroo. She picked up Sammy Snail. She dropped him in her kangaroo pouch.

Soon it was time for the big race. Robby Rabbit and Kami Kangaroo raced together. As they hopped to the finish line, Kami Kangaroo took Sammy Snail out of her pouch. She set him down across the finish line. Sammy Snail won the big race!

Reading Skills

1. What could be another title for this story?

   A. How Sammy Snail Wins the Race

   B. Robby Rabbit Wins the Race

   C. Kami Kangaroo Wins the Race

2. Why was Sammy Snail sad?

   A. He ran too fast.

   B. He was too slow to be in the big race.

   C. He broke his leg.

3. How did Kami Kangaroo help Sammy Snail win the race?

   A. Kami Kangaroo ran backwards.

   B. Kami Kangaroo hid Robby Rabbit.

   C. Kami Kangaroo carried Sammy Snail in her pouch and set him across the finish line.

4. Why was Sammy Snail sad?

_____

_____

_____

_____

5. How did Kami Kangaroo help Sammy Snail?

_____

_____

_____

_____

Vocabulary Skills

1. What is another word for <u>pouch</u>?

_____

_____

Thinking Skills

1. How do you think Sammy Snail felt about winning the race?

_____

_____

_____

_____

Answer Pages

Page 8

Reading Skills
1. A
2. B
3. B

Thinking Skills
1. A

Vocabulary Skills
1. B

Language Skills
1. Sam, cap, has, Max, cat, lap, tan, pats, sand, bag, ran, naps
2. A-Sam, cat; B-tan, ran;
   C-cap, lap; D-nap, sand

Page 10

Reading Skills
1. B
2. A
3. C

Thinking Skills
1. B
2. B

Vocabulary Skills
1. B

Language Skills
1. A-cat, hat; B-can, man; C-cab

Page 12

Reading Skills
1. B
2. C
3. B
4. A
5. B

Thinking Skills
1. The lid might have closed. The box was deep.

Page 14

Reading Skills
1. B
2. T   T   F   T   F   F   T
3. B

Thinking Skills
1. Big Pets: horse, cow, pig, sheep
   Little Pets: cat, dog, mouse, hamster
   (<u>dog</u> might appear in either list)

Vocabulary Skills
1. A

Language Skills
1. Possible Answers:
   Meg, vet, help, pets, mend, pet, pep

Page 16

Reading Skills
1. B
2. 1 pig, 2 hens, 3 chicks, 4 elephant
3. C

Thinking Skills
1. Farm Animals: hen, chick, pig
   Zoo Animals: elephant, giraffe, tiger

Vocabulary Skills
1. B

Language Skills
1. A-who, B-no, C-that

Page 18

Reading Skills
1. A

Language Skills
1. fish   dish
   ship   trip
   chip   dip
   pig   jig

Vocabulary Skills
1. A

Thinking Skills
1. Y
   Y
   Y
   N
2. Answers will vary.

www.summerbridgeactivities.com   Reading Connection—Grade 1—RBP3802

Answer Pages

Page 20

Reading Skills
1. A
2. A

Vocabulary Skills
1. B

Language Skills
1. short <u>e</u> words: hen, ten, pen
   short <u>i</u> words: chicks, pig, in

Page 22

Reading Skills
1. B
2. F   F   T   F

Thinking Skills
1. Answers will vary.

Language Skills
1. A-dog, lot; B-got, rock; C-shop, hot
2. Possible answers include
   lot — hot
   sun — bun
   hound — pound
   me — see

Vocabulary Skills
1. B

Page 24

Reading Skills
1. B
2. A
3. C

Language Skills
1. Bob, cop, stop, job, cross

Thinking Skills
1. Answers will vary.

Page 26

Reading Skills
1. B
2. T   F   F   F
3. A
4. A. man
   B. gold
   C. Pots

Thinking Skills
1. A

Vocabulary Skills
1. A

Page 28

Reading Skills
1. B
2. B
3. A

Thinking Skills
1. Answers will vary.

Vocabulary Skills
1. A

Language Skills
1. pups, cubs, but, run, tug, fun

Page 30

Reading Skills
1. B
2. C, B, D, A, E

Thinking Skills
1. B
2. Answers will vary.

Vocabulary Skills
1. B

Page 32

Reading Skills
1. A

Thinking Skills
1. Bigger Than a Dog: yak, pig, ram
   Smaller Than a Dog: ant, rat, hen

Language Skills
1. short a words: yak, ant, rat, ram, asked, gnat, cat
   short e words: hen, yes
   short o words: dog
   short i words: big, kid, pig, whispered
   short u words: buzzed, sun, clucked

Vocabulary Skills
1. whispered, quacked, barked, buzzed

Page 34

Reading Skills
1. C
2. B
3. A
4. baby, sister, Dad, Grandpa

Thinking Skills
1. Answers will vary.

Vocabulary Skills
1. napping, snoozing

Page 36

Reading Skills
1. B
2. C
3. B

Thinking Skills
1. Toy: choo choo, chopper, checkers
   Not a Toy: checkers, chair, charm
   (checkers may appear in either list)

Vocabulary Skills
1. C

Language Skills
1. thing-bring, chain-rain, air-chair

Page 38

Reading Skills
1. A
2. numbers, math, which path, us, them, her, him, thimbles, thread

Thinking Skills
1. Answers will vary.

Language Skills
1. math   path
   out   about
   thread   head
2. th sound in thin   th sound in then
   math   this
   think   that
   thing   there

Page 40

Vocabulary Skills
1. B

Thinking Skills
1. Answers will vary.
2. A
3. Answers will vary.

Language Skills
1. what, whack, wharf, whine, wheel, whirl, whim, where, wheat, whips, whiskers, whistle, while, whale, whiff, when, white, whispers, which

Page 42

Reading Skills
1. B
2. ducks   quack
   chicks   cheep
   boy   why?
   mouse   squeak
3. 1 ducks, 2 chicks, 3 boy, 4 mouse
4. A. waddled
   B. cat
   C. stopped
   D. scurried

Thinking Skills
1. C

Vocabulary Skills
1. A

Answer Pages

Page 44

Reading Skills
1. B
2. 4, 1, 2, 3
3. A

Thinking Skills
1. Answers will vary.

Vocabulary Skills
1. a_e: cake, race, snake, same
   ay: Gayle, play, day, Jay
   ai: train, sail, tail, trail

Page 46

Reading Skills
1. A
2. B
3. A

Vocabulary Skills
1. C
2. A

Language Skills
1. o_e: hope, froze, note, choke
   oa: boat, road, moat, roast
   old: bold, cold, told, old

Page 48

Reading Skills
1. C
2. A
3. B
4. D

Vocabulary Skills
1. C

Language Skills
2. Duke, dude, mule, rude, tune, cube

Page 50

Reading Skills
1. A
2. June/lute, Hugo/bugle, Judy/flute, Duke/tuba

Language Skills
1. Any of the following: bugle, cute, duet, Duke, flute, huge, Hugo, Judy, July, June, Luke, lutes, music, Ruby, super, Susan, tuba, tune, tutu, uniform.
2. Any of the following: cute, Duke, flute, huge, Hugo, Judy, July, June, Luke, lute(s), music, Ruby, super, Susan, tuba, tune, tutu, uniform
3. duet

Page 52

Reading Skills
1. A
2. C
3. A
4. B

Vocabulary Skills
1. B

Language Skills
1. Dawn, straw, hawk, squawk, claw, brawl, raw, paw, jaw

Page 54

Reading Skills
1. C
2. B
3. B

Thinking Skills
1. C

Language Skills
1. our, ground, around, house

Vocabulary Skills
1. B

Page 56

Reading Skills
1. B
2. C
3. A
4. C

Language Skills
1. oi words: foil   coil   coin
   oy words: boy   Troy   royal

Vocabulary Skills
1. A
2. A

Page 58

Reading Skills
1. make-believe
2. cat fell in the pool   they threw a loop
   goose threw a broom   they ducked
   hen flew the coop   they made soup
   cow jumped over the moon   they laughed

Language Skills
1. ew words: threw   crew   knew
                 blew   flew
   oo words: pool   zoo   loop   broom
                 goose   coop   moon

Vocabulary Skills
1. D
2. B

Page 60

Reading Skills
1. B
2. C
3. C

Vocabulary Skills
1. A
2. C

Language Skills
1. hook, cook, brook, book, wood, soot, foot, shook, took

Page 62

Reading Skills
1. C
2. Who?   Cody
   What?   sailed a boat
   When?   today
   Where?   at the pond
3. soap, rope, paper, stick

Thinking Skills
1. Answers will vary.

Language Skills
1. oa words: soap, toad, float
   o-e words: rope, rope, shore

Vocabulary Skills
1. A

Page 64

Reading Skills
1. B
2. 1, 3, 2

Vocabulary Skills
1. C

Language Skills
1. Jan   Jane   hid   hide
   tap   tape   cub   cube
   pet   Pete   cut   cute
   hop   hope

Page 66

Reading Skills
1. A
2. A
3. B
4. singing, flowers, kite flying, swings

Thinking Skills
1. Answers will vary.

Vocabulary Skills
1. B

Page 68

Reading Skills
1. A
2. ✔: link a chain around a rink,
blink if someone shoots you with ink
clean your mother's mink
   X: drink pink ink
spit on a rink
shrink your mother's mink

Thinking Skills
1. Answers will vary.

Vocabulary Skills
1. drink pink ink blink think
   rink link shrink stinks mink

Language Skills
1. drink pink ink blink think
   rink link shrink stinks mink

Page 70

Thinking Skills
1. Answers will vary.

Vocabulary Skills
1. sea, deer, see, dear
2. flu   flew
   ate   eight
   there   their
   where   wear
   week   weak

Language Skills
1. same   different

Thinking Skills
1. Answers will vary.

Page 72

Reading Skills
1. B
2. Quiet time is only at night when it's really quiet.

Thinking Skills
1. Answers will vary.

Vocabulary Skills
1. it   is
   can   not
   we   are

Page 74

Reading Skills
1. Answers will vary.
2. She wanted to fly her kite.
3. She went up a hill.

Language Skills
1. white, kite

Page 76

Reading Skills
1. She made breakfast.
2. 3, 2, 1, 4
3. jam

Thinking Skills
1. happy, pleased, glad, etc.

Page 78

Reading Skills
1. A

Thinking Skills
1. Answers will vary.

Language Skills
1. long e words: eat   sweet me
                  sleep leap
   long i words: time   fly   rise
                  nice   write light

Vocabulary Skills
1. A

Answer Pages

Page 80

Reading Skills
1. C
2. around   found
   lake   pancake
   cape   grape
   pie   tie
   sunflower   hour

Thinking Skills
1. Answers will vary.

Vocabulary Skills
1. blue/berry   grass/hopper   rain/bow
   Super/man   sun/flower   pan/cake
   mid/night   vine/yard

Page 82

Reading Skills
1. B
2. C
3. B
4. A

Vocabulary Skills
1. A

Thinking Skills
1. B
2. Answers will vary.

Page 84

Reading Skills
1. B
2. ladybug
3. hopped by/grasshopper
   flew onto Katie's hand/ladybug
   pulled a big leaf/ant
   landed on a flower/bee

Thinking Skills
1. Answers will vary.

Page 86

Reading Skills
1. B
2. A
3. 4, 3, 1, 2

Thinking Skills
1. Answers will vary.

Vocabulary Skills
1. B

Page 88

Reading Skills
1. C
2. 4, 1, 2, 3
3. F, T, F, T

Vocabulary Skills
1. A

Page 90

Reading Skills
1. A
2. C
3. 4, 1, 2, 3

Thinking Skills
1. B
2. Answers will vary.

Vocabulary Skills
1. turtle   strolled
   mouse   scampered
   duck   waddled
   rabbit   hopped

©RBP Books   www.summerbridgeactivities.com   Reading Connection—Grade 1—RBP3802

Page 92

Reading Skills
1. Who?   Grayson
   What?   went to find a dragon
   When?   once upon a time
2. A
3. A

Vocabulary Skills
1. B

Thinking Skills
1. B
2. Answers will vary.

Page 94

Reading Skills
1. C
2. Mars   red clay
   Jupiter   moons
   Saturn   rings
3. 4, 3, 1, 2

Vocabulary Skills
1. A, D

Thinking Skills
1. Answers will vary.

Page 96

Reading Skills
1. A
2. F, T, F, T

Thinking Skills
1. Answers will vary.
2. Answers will vary.

Vocabulary Skills
1. B

Page 98

Reading Skills
1. C
2. C
3. two sisters and two brothers

Vocabulary Skills
1. B

Language Skills
1. long a words: cake   take   Gail
   long e words: Lee   me   three

Thinking Skills
1. Answers will vary.

Page 100

Reading Skills
1. A
2. mother   tape
   father   rope
   sister   dime
   brother   kite
3. C
4. B

Thinking Skills
1. B

Vocabulary Skills
1. C

Page 102

Reading Skills
1. A
2. A

Vocabulary Skills
1. sail   boat
   ship   mate
2. A

Thinking Skills
1. Answers will vary.
2. Answers will vary.

Answer Pages

Page 104

Reading Skills
1. C
2. 4, 1, 2, 5, 3
3. C

Vocabulary Skills
1. stir, blend
2. B
3. B

Thinking Skills
1. Answers will vary.

Page 106

Reading Skills
1. B
2. A
3. A
4. call 911, drop and roll, break a window if you have to, stop what you are doing

Thinking Skills
1. Answers will vary.

Page 108

Reading Skills
1. C
2. 5, 1, 2, 4, 3

Language Skills
1. met   said   thought
2. add <u>ed</u>:   asked, buzzed, barked

    double
    consonant: hopped

    add d: tired, chased, moved, settled, smiled

Page 110

Reading Skills
1. A
2. how long seals stay underwater
   facts about horses
   how many rows of teeth a shark has

Thinking Skills
1. Answers will vary.
2. Answers will vary.

Page 112

Reading Skills
1. Riddles can be found in a dictionary.
2. sniffle   cold
   cuddle   hug
   giggle   laugh
   battle   war
3. cold-mold, hug-bug, bee-tree

Thinking Skills
1. Answers will vary.
2. Answers will vary.

Vocabulary Skills
1. A

Page 114

Reading Skills
1. B

Vocabulary Skills
1. C
2. prance, jump, waddle, strut, pace
3. run

Thinking Skills
1. Answers will vary.

www.summerbridgeactivities.com   Reading Connection—Grade 1—RBP3802

Page 116

Reading Skills
1. C
2. A
3. Denise   princess
   Rob   wizard
   Allie   clown
4. B

Thinking Skills
1. Answers will vary.

Page 118

Reading Skills
1. A
2. B
3. C
4. He wanted to be in a race.
5. She helped him win the race

Vocabulary Skills
1. pocket

Thinking Skills
1. He was happy. He was thankful for a good friend.

Notes

Five things I'm thankful for:

1. _____
2. _____
3. _____
4. _____
5. _____